CULTIVATING A LIFE OF PRAYER

Shout with Joy
to Our God !

Yvonne Hebert
5/17/16

CULTIVATING A LIFE OF PRAYER

A HANDBOOK OF LIFE PRACTICES

Yvonne C. Hebert

Books by Yvonne C. Hebert, M.A.

Finding Peace in Pain – 1984, 2015

Room for Another Heart – 2012, 2015
A novel about people, dogs, and all things forest

Rethinking Forgiveness – 2013, 2015
Mental Tactics to Avoid Resentment

Cultivating a Life of Prayer– 2015
A Handbook of Life Practices

Rethinking Forgiveness for Christians – 2015
Prayer Supports and Mental Tactics to Avoid Resentment

This book may be ordered through Amazon, Barnes & Noble, booksellers, and directly from the author at colliehouse@aol.com, **wwwyvonnehebert.com**

ISBN: 13-978-1512273687
ISBN: 10-1512273686

Library of Congress Control Number: Pending
Printed in the United States of America

Psalm 34

I will bless Yahweh at all times,
His praise shall be on my lips continually;
My soul glories in Yahweh,
Let the humble hear and rejoice.

Proclaim with me the greatness of Yahweh,
Together let us extol his name.
I seek Yahweh, and he answers me
And frees me from all my fears.

Every face turned to him grows brighter
And is never ashamed.
A cry goes up from the poor man, and Yahweh hears,
And helps him in all his troubles.

The angel of Yahweh pitches camp
Around those who fear him; and he keeps them safe.
How good Yahweh is – only taste and see!
Happy the person who takes shelter in him.

Psalm 34:1-10

Contents

Acknowledgements

Many years ago, I talked extensively with Rev. John Kane, C.Ss.R., Founder and Director of the Desert House of Prayer in Cortaro, Arizona until his passing in 2001. Much of the following material are ways that he taught me to develop my prayer life.

In earlier years, I had listened closely and studied the lectures given by Rev. John H. Hampsch, CMF, which added to the depth of my understanding of spirituality and prayer.

Rev. Al Scott, of Long Beach, Ca. demonstrated verbally and through the way he lives his life, his belief that balance and discipline were requisites for having the strength to pursue a life of prayer and spiritual development.

Sr. Julia Costello of the Daughters of Mary and Joseph shared a gentle but probing listening skill and a belief in the power of Icons and personal artistic creativity to help pinpoint areas where personal work was needed as well as an inspirational passage for getting in touch with the Divine.

I am deeply grateful for their patience with me and their willingness to support my efforts to understand the need for prayer, creativity, balance, and discipline in one's life.

There are, oh, so many other people, too numerous to mention, who have inspired me with their lives of prayer, of duty, of temperance, and of perseverance in the face of difficulty. I owe all of them a debt of gratitude for their example on how to live a life of prayer and Christian love.

Yvonne C. Hebert
July, 2015

Preface

This book details a compendium of various supports for encouraging a spiritual life of extra-ordinary devotion. There's no Latin anywhere in this book! No 10-syllable words that carry an encyclopedia of meanings and a doctorate in theology to understand. This is a book written by a layperson for a layperson.

As noted in the Acknowledgements, I have become aware of these practices from a number of sources I learned to hold in high esteem because I saw these people living the life they taught.

I would like to say that I do all of the exercises I am about to detail for you every day, but I can't. I can say that I have used them all and that each of these supports, alone or in combination, have been important to my spiritual maturation. I also go back to those practices I don't do regularly when I feel sluggish in my prayer life. Without fail, I am rewarded with new insights about Jesus Christ and energized in my faith. It is for that reason that I want to pass them on to you.

I believe that as I tried each of these activities I became more aware of the awesome power of prayer and the need to keep working at understanding more and more about the Presence of Almighty God in our daily lives and habits.

Relationships take time and attention. As a psychologist, I know that. I preach it to my clients constantly. You can't love someone you don't know with the intensity that you love someone with whom you are intimate.

What I've had to learn at a deeply personal level is that a relationship with Jesus Christ falls into that same pattern – to know Him is to love Him, but to know him deeply and personally is to love Him intensely.

That decision takes time and attention and the strength to persevere in that effort. Knowing God -- Creator, Savior, Spirit -- in a deeply personal way is worth that effort and beyond words to describe fully.

And that's why I'm writing this little book.

Yvonne C. Hebert

July, 2015

1 *MAKING THE DECISION*

Is it Time for Your Prayer Life
To Become a Life of Prayer?

Has your prayer life become a comfortable ritual with which you feel vaguely dissatisfied? Have you felt Jesus calling you to a greater depth of prayer but you haven't been quite sure what to do to deepen your relationship with Him?

There are many avenues to a deeper relationship with Jesus but the first step is to want it. A life of prayer makes demands on the individual's body, time, and activities in ways that a prayer life does not.

The second step is to move forward gradually, not stressing yourself or feeling like you have to make many changes instantly. Some practices many seem very easy to add to your prayer life but some may take years to master. It may feel that there isn't enough time in the day to fit some suggestions into your life. That is the way it should be – for now.

As you develop an attitude of living a life with Jesus constantly in your thoughts and the desire to know him more personally than you ever have before, the movement toward Him will become ever easier.

When we feel this restless calling to a very close walk with Our Lord, there are decisions we need to make and activities we need to add to our lifestyle to enable us to live in a manner conducive to developing an extra-ordinary prayer life.

Let's talk about each of them in more detail.

2 *God's Athletes*

If we are to lead a life of prayer, we are in need of a finely tuned body. We should consider ourselves God's Athletes! A proper diet, daily exercise, and adequate sleep are basic necessities. Deep prayer takes energy. Energy requires strength.

If our bodies are allowed to deteriorate physically, the human attention span becomes too short to pray in the manner we desire if we are living a life of prayer. Our body is physical, human, functioning. We need to maintain ourselves in as perfect a condition as possible if we are to derive the necessary support from our bodies for the life of prayer we want to live.

If we find that our bodies are not as finely tuned as we wish they were, we need to develop a schedule of eating, sleeping, and exercise so that we will, in time, reach our goal. That schedule should include daily morning prayer during which we ask God to provide us with the wisdom to know what in our life needs to change in order to reach our goal and the strength to persevere in those changes.

Over time, we may see that our lives become more ordered and less stressed. Disorder now feels burdensome and we may find that we find pleasure in doing the small chores of living that once seemed onerous but now seem to keep our lives in balance.

It is difficult to maintain a healthy mind and spirit in a neglected physical body. Taking the time necessary to keep our body toned, properly fed, and rested becomes an ordinary discipline.

Most people need seven or eight hours of sleep every night. Twenty minutes in the afternoon for meditation or some rest can leave a person feeling refreshed, mentally sharp, and better able to cope with the stresses of the day. Remember that even the Trappists allow themselves seven hours of sleep every day.

It isn't just athletes that need exercise. Everyone needs daily conditioning appropriate for what they are physically able to do. People with sedentary jobs are especially vulnerable to evening fatigue and the desire to be a couch potato. Drink a glass of water and take a leisurely walk for a few minutes to stimulate the desire to exercise. During the day take a break from sitting every hour. Stand at your desk while you talk on the telephone or walk for a few minutes.

Keep in mind that law of physics: A body in motion tends to stay in motion, a body at rest tends to stay at rest. Push for that burst of energy to change the pattern you are in. The human body was constructed for movement. Lack of movement presages decay.

Food intake is very personal but everyone knows the foods that agree with them and those that don't. For a moment, think of your body as a finely-tuned car. You wouldn't put saltwater or mayonnaise in your car and expect it to run. Don't do something similar to your body. It was created to run on veggies, fruit, and protein. To demand that it function well on sugary treats and potato chips is unreasonable. Take the time to eat properly.

I have to admit that I have taken an unusual perspective on eating. If it's a prepared food from the store, I offer some of it to my dogs. If they won't eat it, neither will I. Sometimes I will take some and set it out for the birds and chipmunks around my house.

Generally speaking, if my dogs won't eat it, neither will they. This has eliminated potato chips, salted crackers, prepared popcorn, margarines, and many other foods from my diet. I've learned that sometimes I can trick my dogs by adding cheese to these products but they rarely fall for that ploy twice. I was amazed to see that even ants and birds will ignore these "foods."

A friend once put a lid with margarine on it and a second lid with butter on it outside on her front lawn. The next day the butter was swarming with outdoor bugs, ants, and winged insects but the margarine was untouched. Two weeks later the margarine lid was still pristine shiny. It seemed to me that nature was teaching us a serious lesson and I needed to pay attention.

Impulsive Behavior:

If you are praying for strength to persevere in changing some personal habits but find that you continue to fail in your efforts, consider the following suggestion.

In response to preferred temptations, sometimes people behave impulsively. Science has learned that *thoughts that could help us resist such temptations are much slower to surface cognitively and are weak compared to the strength of the impulsive response.*

Giving in to the impulsive response can lead to feelings of guilt and inadequacy, and it can interfere with our feeling of being "good enough" to attempt to attain a state of holiness.

Cognitive training which requires the brain to stretch its memory ability and to think quickly and flexibly appears to be part of a solution. If you decide that you need this type of training, keep in mind that it has to be varied in content and design. There should be no upper limits so that the individual is able to continue to stretch their mental capacity.

Coupled with response inhibition training techniques, current studies show promise in helping impulsive people gain control over temptations and has been gaining acceptance in scientific circles lately. [1]

Putting the above suggestions into practice may require the individual to work at memory building and flexibility exercises which can be found on various computer sites. Response inhibition training is not as easily accessed by individuals, since it is still in its research infancy. A person can create their own response inhibition program by asking friends to support their effort to change and by instituting response delay techniques into their daily lives.

One practice that can slow down your response is to make it a habit to say a Hail Mary before doing the activity that you are trying to change. Ask the Blessed Mother to intervene and help keep you on track to your desired goal. Such a practice will also help to develop a more loving relationship between yourself and Our Lady. She is an incredibly powerful spiritual ally to have in your life!

Another would be to wait 15 minutes before doing what you want to do and spending those minutes questioning yourself as to why you wish to give in to that temptation at that particular time. There could also be an emotional component which you may need to confront to successfully make the change you want to make.

Keep in mind that you are paying attention to the needs of your body because you are human as well as spiritual. Your brain is part of your human body and may need impulse control training much the same way as your muscles need to be trained.

It's worth noting that we do have control of our thoughts. We can think the thoughts we want to think. *Our thoughts do not have control of us, we have control of our thoughts.* We can choose the thoughts we want to think, and ponder the thoughts we want to think about more deeply. We do not have to allow any thought that enters our mind to take root and influence our mood or behavior.

Keep in mind that our brains are very busy places with work to do every second of our lives. For our brain to take a siesta could mean our demise. There are neurons firing; blood flowing through vessels; chemicals making their way to receptor sites; a flurry of constant action which keeps our brain cells alive and functioning. The more we stimulate our brain, the more efficient it becomes.

Sometimes our thoughts are well ordered and serve to help us understand our environment or find successful ways to communicate. Sometimes our thoughts are a surprise to us, with ideas popping in unbidden, with memories surfacing and feelings stirred up that we would just as soon leave forgotten.

At times we may be astounded at a memory which flashes through our mind and we wonder why that particular memory surfaced at that particular time. It serves us well to keep in mind that every experience, every feeling, every sight, every smell, we've ever had is recorded in our brain for all time.

Unless we suffer from a brain-wasting disease where structures of our brain actually disintegrate, every memory can be tapped by the stimulation of the brain where that memory is stored.

Through the random activity of our brain going on in the background of our consciousness, we may suddenly find ourselves thinking thoughts or experiencing feelings from the past at times we'd rather not be reminded of them. At such times, these thoughts and feelings can stimulate impulsive behaviors to comfort or to distract ourselves from these unwanted thoughts and feelings.

No one has to react impulsively to any stimuli or random thought that pops into their mind. To distract yourself from a thought you do not wish to have, do whatever you can do physically: pet the dog, call a friend, bake a cake, read a book, take a shower, touch your toes a few times, or tell yourself: "I wonder where that thought (or feeling) came from. I'd rather think about the flowers I plan to plant in the garden next spring." Then actively start planning your garden.

If you want a foolproof method of distracting yourself quickly from any thought, start counting backwards from 100 (or 1,000). It's especially difficult to count backwards by an odd number such as 7. The part of your mind that does math is in a totally different area than memories. You cannot think of both math and memories at the same time.

Balance is another area of the brain that is in a different area than thought processes. You cannot put yourself in an activity where you must keep yourself physically balanced and think about anything else. In college, our instructor advised our counseling class to run on curbs, or to run on and jump from one parking lot stanchion to the next, until our minds cleared and we felt happy and excited about life again. As I've gotten older and less mobile, I've learned that walking cross-legged across the floor, first in one direction, and then in the other, is also an excellent balancing exercise.

Note that I am not suggesting prayer at such a time but rather activities that involve physical movement, math, or interaction with another person or the ideas of another person. This could be a good time for spiritual reading or praying the psalms or other written prayers. It is a time when you need to stimulate a different part of your brain than memory. Spontaneous prayer would, in all likelyhood, continue the activity in the same part of the brain as memory causing a confusing and distracting medley of thoughts.

Just remember, your mind will go along with whatever you tell it to think about. Teach yourself to think the way you want to think. You are not at the mercy of your mind's efforts to exercise itself. The more practice you get at controlling the focus of your mind, the more easily you will be able to direct your attention where you want it to go.

[1] Houben, K., Wiers, R.W., and Jansen, A. (2011) University of Amsterdam, *Getting a Grip on Drinking Behavior: Training Working Memory to Reduce Alcohol Abuse,* Psychological Science Abstract: www.ncbi.nem.gov/pubmed/21685380

3   *The Work We Do*

Our work lives also need to be in harmony with our prayer goals. The work we do can affect our peace of mind if it is frustrating to us. If we are under-employed or over-employed, we may suffer boredom or stress that can cause us to question our purpose in life. We should attempt to find work that is personally rewarding to us and uses the talents God has given us.

Since such work is not always available, we need to make efforts to reach a place of peace with the work we do have. Remember that St. Paul earned his livelihood as a tentmaker!

In the event that we seem unable to find work in a satisfying position, it becomes very important to find rewarding alternatives for the hours we are not working.

It is usual to find that God will use all of our education and experience for His purposes. If we find ourselves in a frustrating work situation, we should continue to look for opportunities which will use our talents while maintaining peace with ourselves in our present situation.

In my own life, I have found myself in work situations where I have been most unhappy. But each time that I was able to trust that God had a purpose for me in that distasteful situation, I would soon recognize that there was something or someone there who needed to be touched by my personal faith and talents. Amazingly, the need would soon be resolved and I would move on to happier circumstances.

In one situation I was contracted as a consultant for a specific time period and couldn't get out of the contract. I found myself working in an atmosphere of heavy political in-fighting, a brazen lack of ethics, and an introverted department head who didn't want to deal with the problems of his staff. I realized rather quickly why they needed a consultant!

In a matter of days I was praying for God's help in getting me out of this position. Two weeks later a new secretary was hired who shared with me that she was a Christian and appalled at the milieu of the department.

Together we formed a bond and supported each other for several months until my work was completed and I was able to leave. A week later she called to tell me that another department had suddenly hired her and she was transferring at the end of the week.

I saw this as a direct answer to prayer. God provided me with support while I had to be there to accomplish work that was needed for the community at large. God protected the person he had sent to support me by arranging a transfer for her as soon as I was gone.

Make no mistake: God is personal and powerful.

4   *The Diversions We Enjoy*

Diversions from our daily schedule are necessary every day. The person devoutly leading a life of prayer must have command of the diversions which they enjoy and to which they are exposed. Some activities and some people are not conducive to furthering our prayer goals and some situations can be dangerous to our spiritual lives. As we get ever closer to our still point in prayer, we will know what we need to pare out of our lives and what can remain.

As we consider possible diversions, it is important to remember that human beings are more than mind and spirit. We are also physical beings and we need to take our bodies and its needs into consideration as we determine what our diversions will be.

- Physical activities such as sports can be an exhilarating break from our normal routine.
- Physical movement in itself can bring us great joy.
- Engaging our creative side with some form of artistic or musical venture can help us open up hidden interests and can be very enjoyable even if our talents and skills are quite ordinary.

- The study of religious Icons can stimulate our understanding of the Divine and the artist's effort to share their vision.

- Spending time in community service to others less fortunate than ourselves helps to develop virtues of compassion and generosity while expanding our knowledge of the world around us.

- Enrolling in a nearby college or university for classes that interest us can keep our minds agile and our knowledge base current.

- Sharing meals and conversation with like-minded people is always a stimulating as well as refreshing diversion from our everyday lives.

As our prayer life deepens and we develop an understanding of what diversions are good for us, there are some points we should consider.

In today's world, there is great emphasis on excesses of all kinds. "More is better" seems to be the world view and unrestrained boundaries give way to even greater extremes.

There is a reason for this. When daily living causes us stress and overload, we begin to reach a place where we cease to feel alive. Excitement causes us to feel our emotions, but we soon adapt to that level of sensation. To feel alive, we need ever increasing levels of greater and stronger excitement. This leads us into a state of addiction to whatever form of excitement has been our choice.

If we stop our addiction, we feel empty. Peaceful, calm feelings have become too tame. In fact, they may actually feel unpleasant to a person who has become addicted to thrills, emotionalism or a sense of urgency.

For those of us who have been this route and emerged with a desire for a closer union with God, our histories can cause us to doubt our sincerity at times. Even when we control our addiction, the desire for excitement may surface without warning.

I noticed that this often occurred to me during prayer or at Mass. This was very unsettling. It made me think my efforts to pray were not from my heart, but intellectually I knew better. On a physical level, such random thoughts come from the brain.

Our brain is an incredibly powerful and fascinating part of our body. Scientists have learned that stimulating different parts of the human brain during surgeries trigger memories that the patient believed they had forgotten long ago. It has become an accepted belief that nothing we experience is ever forgotten as long as our brains are functioning.

Therefore, we need to protect our brains from sights, sounds, smells, and actions that will stimulate us in ways that do not bring peace. This includes movies, music, pictures, other objects, and activities that we can listen to or view. If our senses experience something, we have a memory of it. We do not have to physically experience something for our minds to remember the event.

While this may seem to have little impact on an individual's daily life, for the person who is striving to develop a life of prayer, it can be a problem.

It may take a long time for violent, gross, or erotic memories and/or habits to recede into the background and stop bothering us. If you should experience such a disturbance, pray harder. Don't allow your thoughts to distract you from your goal. Pray for the strength to persevere in your efforts to pray always.

A rule of thumb that you can count on forever is, if you don't want to pray, pray! If you feel an aversion to prayer or wanting to pray, pray as if your life depends on prayer, because it does!

On a spiritual level, the devil knows you very well. It is acquainted with you and your personal history and has the ability to suggest thoughts to you that will distract you from prayer. If you give in every time the devil tempts you, it has no reason to stop trying to pull you back to your old life. If every time you are tempted, you draw closer to God the devil will leave you alone. It hates to lose and a soul devoted to God is a loss for the devil.

5 *Relationships with Other People*

Our relationships with other people will give us an indication of how our prayer life is developing. As a person progresses toward God, a sensitive feeling is developed for others. The love we feel from Jesus and for Jesus finds its way into our interactions with other people.

Prejudices fall away. Fear vanishes. Generosity blossoms. Our compassion increases. Judging and controlling others becomes unnecessary. Our prayer life helps us to have peace and a universal love in our relationships with the people around us.

This doesn't mean that we become passive observers of life dominated by others. It is important that others know when we believe our culture is out of step with the commandments of God. It does mean that others perceive that we are living our lives with joy and purpose and they can feel safe in our presence.

As our awareness and generosity toward other people expands so also does our willingness to pray for them and for their needs. We become deeply aware of the power of prayer and the personal impact it can have in our own life and the lives of others.

When we pray for people we are moving into Intercessory Prayer for their needs. Bring as clear a picture as possible of the person into your mind as you pray for them, and attempt to pray for their needs with energy, emotion, and expectant faith.

Pray for them with the knowledge that God loves them, loves you, and wants the very best for both of you. Picture them healthy, happy, and praising God for their blessings. Praying this way will not only be beneficial for them, it will also fill your own heart with peace about their situation.

Anxiety

We find ourselves living peacefully while others around us may be subject to periods of deep anxiety and fear. The reality of God's awesome power has penetrated our souls.

We understand that living in fear and expressing anxiety about cultural changes and evil practices in the world does not bring glory to God but does draw attention to the devil's designs.

Living in anxiety spreads a helpless kind of energy which creates fear and confusion in others. Anxiety can be paralyzing and depressing to ourselves and to those around us. If we spend our time and energy emotionally attacking the evil of the devil, we are not free to devote our energies to fostering an understanding of the power and love of God.

We know that the Scriptures repeatedly tell us that God has said, "Fear Not, for I am your God." "Do not be afraid" is a command, not a suggestion, and can be found in many places in the

CULTIVATING A LIFE OF PRAYER

Bible. To name a few: Psalms 37:1- 7; 43:5; Isaiah 41:10; Matthew 6:31-34; Philippians 4:6-9; 2 Thessalonians 3:3; and 1 Peter 5:7.

As we develop trust in God's plans for us and for this world we are able to speak logically and forcefully for social justice in all of its aspects.

We can foster peace through dialogue instead of violence or emotional tirades. We can respect each other's journey to God.

Eliminating anxiety from our hearts allows our focus to become a positive energy that builds hope and encourages others to believe as we do..

Forgiveness

Another aspect of relationship is the development of an attitude of forgiveness. Forgiveness is a primary concern in relationships with others. When we have felt insulted or neglected by people, especially those important to us, feelings of anger or resentment can be very quick to surface.

For our peace of mind and maturation as a Christian, forgiving ourselves and others is imperative – and the sooner, the better.

Hard as this may be to believe, forgiveness is not a concept practiced only by Christians. Religious leaders, teachers, and philosophers throughout the ages, and from every continent in the world, have cautioned their followers to forgive others in order to live peacefully.

The Psalms, The Book of Wisdom, and other books of the Old Testament speak often of leaving vengeance to the Lord God, and finding peace in forgiving others.

Hundreds of years before Jesus Christ, Socrates, Confucius, and Budda were preaching the doctrine of forgiving self and others. More recently, Nelson Mandela, a political prisoner for 27 years, is quoted as saying, "Resentment is like drinking poison, hoping it will kill your enemies."

There is a Biblical, unilateral basis for forgiveness and for not judging others – even those people who have hurt us. In John 7:7 we read the words of Jesus to the crowd wishing to stone the woman caught in adultery. "If there is one of you who has not sinned, let him be the first to throw a stone at her."

Forgiving is hard. Whether you are trying to forgive yourself or someone else, it's still really hard. Forgiveness is surely one of the most difficult challenges in life, but perhaps that's because we don't understand what it means to forgive.

Forgiveness isn't some kind of gift we give an abuser. It isn't letting someone who has insulted us get away with their violence. It isn't allowing ourselves to be degraded, humiliated, or injured without any attempt at defense. It isn't giving an abuser a superior position to ourselves.

It's breaking the emotional ties between the two of you that have been created by your emotional reaction to the insult you have perceived. It is putting the responsibility for the situation squarely on the shoulders of the person who created it.

Many people won't even know they did anything to upset you. They don't even know they need forgiving. They are continuing on with their lives while you live with resentment, perhaps even acting out some of your negative feelings on people with whom you come in contact.

You need to make the decision to forgive offensive behavior in other people because you deserve to live in peace. Forgiving breaks the emotional chains that tie you to resentment over the behavior of another person.

Even when a person has deliberately offended you, the responsibility for their behavior rests with them. The abusive type of person seems to kindle a fire in their victims for revenge or at least an apology.

The person devoted to a life of prayer will recognize that the abusive person is acting out an emotional immaturity that has nothing to do with their victim.

The emotional maturation required for sincere apologies, the desire to live in harmony and equality with others, and the ability to change, only happen with a personal awareness which develops over a long period of time in most individuals. It also takes work on the part of the individual, and many people do not want to invest that kind of energy into changing themselves. They may feel they are living the way they want to live and see no benefit for themselves in making the effort to change.

Waiting for another person to mature emotionally and change their ways before you allow yourself to find peace of mind is risking your happiness for a very long time – perhaps your entire lifetime!

Releasing people who have offended you to their own conscience can bring a peacefulness to the person who is developing an attitude of forgiveness.

The time to start the process of forgiveness is before you have been insulted. Take a moment each morning to ask God for the wisdom and the serenity to bring peace to those you meet and to the situations you will encounter during the day.

Pray for the grace to maintain control of your passions until you have had the time to reflect on how you desire to act. Pray that your response will bring honor to your discipleship as a follower of Jesus and enlightenment to those around you.

Understand that while it is important for you to forgive the transgressions of others and your own imperfect behavior, there is no requirement that you tolerate abuse from other people.

Our relationships should support our ambition to be Heaven-bound. The relationships we foster during our lifetime should be supportive of our Christian ideals. Presumably, these friendships and family members will help us become more Christ-like, more peace-loving, more mature as Christians.

If we have stumbled into a relationship with someone who leaves us feeling depressed, combative, angry, vengeful, willing to behave with questionable morality to keep their affection, or to engage in questionable ethics to accommodate their behavior, we are moving away from Jesus, not closer to him.

When we realize the ramifications of knowing such a person, we need to consider how our bond with them is affecting our eternal destiny – and theirs.

The Biblical directive that we "love others as we love ourselves" does not imply that we love others *more* than ourselves. It does not imply that we allow ourselves to be abused by another person or that we need to support them in sinful behaviors.

We need to discuss with them the error of their ways in a gentle and loving manner. If we don't, we are allowing them to continue in sinful ways without bringing attention to their behavior which can only be displeasing to God. Their souls are at stake for all eternity.

If we are unable to speak to such a person about their chosen patterns, we need to have others help us confront them and support them in a change of behavior. If they refuse to listen, the Bible instructs us to pray for them but to end their influence on our lives.[2]

Our choices during our lifetime on this earth have to keep the big picture in focus – and the big picture includes developing our spirituality in accord with God's plan for us to join Him in Heaven for all eternity.

I would recommend taking the time to study my book "Rethinking Forgiveness for Christians" for the details on how to proceed with difficult forgiveness problems. Forgiveness is a topic that cannot be dealt with adequately here, but answers are available.

As a person develops in a life of prayer, they will find the need to be affected by the opinions of others less and less important as they recognize they are truly trying to keep their covenant with God. They fulfill the requirements of citizenship, of friendship, of loyalty, and of service to others, as well as becoming more visible as a positive Christian light before others.

Gossip

A major significant signal that we are progressing in our spiritual journey is a change in our desire to gossip negatively about the people in our lives. There is a difference between sharing positive and happy news about our friends and finding fault with them behind their backs.

There is a positive aspect to discerning poor behavior among our friends in that it helps to bring awareness of the behaviors that we should not be doing because of the hurt it causes others. Sharing can bring help to our friends who need support but are reticent to ask for it. These are very delicate matters and such sharing should be done with prayer, wisdom, and gentleness.

[2] Matt. 18:15-17 and 2Cor.6:14-18

6   *Our Place of Prayer*

As we pray throughout the day, we will find ourselves in many different places and circumstances, but we need to find a space where we can encounter God privately and serenely for our times of personal prayer. This location should, if possible, be the same place every day so that we do not have to re-adjust our senses every day to new surroundings. It should be a serene area with no interruptions and not cluttered with distracting items, noises, or people.

Praying in a chapel in front of the Blessed Sacrament is an ideal place to feel the peace of silence and space. Since chapels are not available to most of us most of the time, an alternative location would be a place where, ideally, we can allow our body position to be inspired without observation by others.

For instance, if we wished to pray prostrated on the floor or wished to sing our prayers of praise to God, we could do so without alarming or embarrassing others. Each of us is so unique that a place to pray that would be perfect for one person may not fit another person's needs.

It may be necessary to experiment with different locations until the place most conducive for us to pray is found, and then we should pray there as much as possible.

Even at Sunday Mass, we may find ourselves less distracted and more inclined to pray attentively if we sit in the same area each week.

Our body adjusts to events that take place at regular intervals – even spaced a week or more apart. Striving to give our physical senses less to focus on allows our minds the energy to more effectively concentrate on our prayers.

7 *Length of Time in Prayer*

The length of time we are willing to devote to prayer greatly influences the development of one's life of prayer. A pattern of prayer that we follow each month, as well as a schedule we follow each day, helps to keep our progress steady even in periods of depression or dryness.

On a daily basis, we need to start with the amount of time that seems possible for us and build on it throughout our lives. It is better to spend 15 minutes in prayer than not to have a prayer time at all. While we are being drawn more deeply in love with Jesus, we will think of Him more often throughout the day. Finding ourselves talking to Him spontaneously builds on those precious moments which we have carved out of our lives to sit quietly with Him.

As we move through various stages of prayer we will want to be protective of our time with Him. When we begin to practice meditative and contemplative prayer, an hour passes very quickly since it takes time to settle down, to find one's still point, and have time for prayer.

Setting aside 4 to 5 hours each month for a special time of reflection about one's progress and goals is very helpful to keep focused on this chosen path toward holiness. This is a good time to read over our spiritual journals to determine if a pattern of action or thought has surfaced and what its implications for our spiritual life might be.

Another practice which can help our life of prayer is to observe Sundays, or a particular Sunday each month, as a day of rest, of prayer, and of contemplation. On this Sunday, it is preferable not to work even about the house, and to shut off forms of communication such as telephones, television, radio, and dates with friends or relatives. A strict diet or fast is also helpful.

Whatever pattern of prayer one chooses, it should be scheduled into our lives as rigidly as the hours we dedicate to sleep. Our prayer time becomes an oasis of strength for us and we may find that the hours moving toward that precious time pass much too slowly.

8 *A Regular Time of Prayer*

A regular time for an extended period of prayer is essential. We need to make an iron clad decision when this time will be, or prayer will become the last thing we try to fit into our day and may be missed. There are various points of view as to when this time should be.

Many spiritual people feel that one's prayer time, to be truly effective, should start the day. There are several reasons for this.

- The mind is often just too busy at night to really relax enough to pray.

- At night people are often too tired to pray and they will gradually slip out of the habit of daily prayer.

- Prayer which starts the day can affect everything that we do during the day.

- As the prayer of quiet is reached, the peace will go with us throughout our activities, perhaps for many hours, and will have an effect on the people that we encounter during the day.

A lengthy morning prayer isn't right for everyone, however. Some folks wake with the concerns of the day facing them and find themselves pulled quickly into the life of their families or professions. At night when the day's duties are clearly finished they can relax and enter into a state of quiet conducive to prayer.

Other people find their lunch break the perfect time to pull apart from others with a protected time to encounter their Lord. Each person needs to find the time of day that feels right for them.

Usually it works best to have a regular pattern of prayer at various times during the day. A brief time of prayer in the morning, afternoon, and evening, with one of those times gradually developing over a period of time into a more lengthy conversation with their Redeemer is popular with many very busy people.

If you don't know when to pray, ask Jesus to schedule your prayer time for you. Then remain open to becoming aware of the time of day when you have the strongest desire to remain in prayer.

9 *Relax During Prayer*

Allowing our body and mind to free itself of tensions and stress will help us to pray. There are a number of calming methods which will help the individual to settle down and relax. Using methods that are strictly for relaxation can be appropriate since we are using these methods to enhance our prayer time.

Two very effective methods to relax are:

The Breathing Method

- Sit with the back straight,
- Feet placed flat on the floor,
- Do not cross your arms or legs as this will hinder circulation.
- Hands should be allowed to rest in one's lap,
- Do not intertwine your fingers as this will hinder circulation.
- Allow your head to rest against the back of your chair or to incline slightly toward your chest.
- Close your eyes.
- Focus on your breathing.
- Feel your breath coming in and going out.

- Your abdomen should swell as you breathe in and deflate as you breathe out.

- Tell the muscles in your face to relax as you breathe in and out

- Tell the muscles in your neck to relax as you breathe in and out.

- Tell your chest muscles to relax as you breathe in and out.

- Tell your upper arm muscles to relax as you breathe in and out.

- Continue through each muscle group in your body, arms, legs and feet until you feel relaxed and your breathing is slow and restful.

- When you feel relaxed and your breathing is restful, start your prayer.

- As you finish your prayer time, sit quietly. Do not rise suddenly. Your balance will be compromised after such intense relaxation. Look around the room, wiggle your fingers and feet until you are fully aware.

- When you stand, move slowly and deliberately.

- Take your peace with you as you leave your place of prayer and go about your life.

The Focusing Method

- Sit quietly in a chair, back and legs straight with feet flat on the floor, hands relaxed in your lap.

- Look at something in the room without moving your head. It could be a crucifix, a flower, a crack in the wall, a pattern in the carpet. Whatever is available to your eyes.

- Obviously, in a time of prayer, the more uplifting and spiritual the object, the more conducive it will be to your prayer.

- Allow yourself to breathe quietly as you focus all your attention on this item.

- As thoughts occur to you, allow them to float out of your mind, keep your visual attention focused on the object you have chosen.

- As your thought processes slow down, begin your prayer.

- As you finish your prayer time, sit quietly. Do not rise quickly. Your balance will be compromised after such intense relaxation. Look around the room, wiggle your fingers and feet until you are fully aware.

- When you stand, move slowly and deliberately.

- Take your peace with you as you leave your place of prayer and go about your life.

With either method, background music that is soft, instrumental, and spiritually uplifting can be played. For some people, background music is an aid in relaxing; for others it can be distracting. Do what works the best for you.

It is not uncommon to find a way to relax that works, and then experience a time when your body and mind remain active and disrupt your prayer time. That could signify a problem surfacing in your life that needs to be attended to spiritually.

If this happens, lift your life to God and ask for His peace with the problems you are experiencing. Share what you think is the problem distracting you and ask for God's wisdom in handling it.

Journal about this problem and what you think God may be telling you about yourself or your problem. Chances are that you will be dealing with this problem over time and will want to remember the insights you have had in the past.

10 Some Stages of Prayer

I think Jesus calls us to change the way we pray at times. Perhaps He's telling us that we are praying too fast and we need to think more about the words we're reading in our formal prayer times. Maybe we need to add our own spontaneous prayers to the formal prayers we may be saying.

If we've become reliant on spontaneous prayers, perhaps our prayer time has become a time of questioning the meaning of our life and asking for help. Perhaps we've become lax in other aspects of prayer: Thanksgiving for what God is doing in our lives, Praise and adoration of God, and expressing our concern for our sins.

It's also possible that we need to become more aware of His actual and attentive presence with us when we pray. Prayer is communication with God. If we think of it as a conversation with Jesus, it becomes apparent that while we may be sitting quietly in our bedroom or car or wherever, we are not alone. Conversation takes at least two people to participate.

Perhaps we've forgotten that anywhere we pray becomes sacred space because Jesus is present there with us. Our prayer may change significantly if we acknowledge to ourselves the reality of His presence with us.

Christians of all denominations may realize they need to spend more time in church activities, such as the Missions, Bible studies, volunteer positions, soup kitchens, or prayer groups throughout the week.

Many people mention that they "talk" to God all day long. They share with Jesus their ideas and concerns about all the events of their lives, their frustrations and annoyances, their joys and the fun things that happen to them. Their travel concerns and their worries about their loved ones are often part of their constant dialogue with God.

Such people may find themselves drawn to the Liturgy of the Hours, the official prayer of the church offered at particular times of the day. While clergy and religious have a church law requirement to pray the Liturgy of the Hours, it is a prayer form freely chosen by much of the laity.

The inspiration for this prayer form seems to have had its origins as an inspiration from the Old Covenant when readings from the Torah, psalms, and hymns replaced the initial bloody sacrifices of morning and evening. In Psalm 119:164 David says "Seven times a day I praise you." In Psalm 1:2 "the just man meditates on the law day and night" would also inspire repeated prayers throughout the day.

St. Benedict devised a program of prayers divided into Lauds (sunrise), Prime (the 1st hour), Terce (mid-morning), Sext (midday), None (mid-afternoon), Vespers (evening), and Compline (night). The Liturgy has followed these divisions throughout the centuries and has been relatively unchanged since the 11th century.

Praying the Liturgy of the Hours is a way of sanctifying one's day and speeds the development of one's spiritual understandings. It brings the individual into the communal prayer of the church and keeps one's prayer in tune with the various feasts and church seasons. It is regarded as a powerful prayer and a definite step toward holiness.

Catholics may discern that it is time to add Masses to their prayer life in addition to Sunday. In times past, very few people lived closed enough to a church to attend Mass during the week no matter how much they might have desired to be there.

Today, with the advent of Eternal Word Television Network, it is possible to attend daily Mass aired at various times during the day. Special Masses from the Vatican and various Basilica's are featured for special feast days. Additionally many cities have Sunday Masses televised in their regions on local channels for those unable to physically attend Mass in their parish.

Adding an artistic endeavor may allow us to creatively explore our spiritual life. Taking up the study of Spiritual Icons may bring a fresh perspective to our spiritual understanding of the Scriptures. Attempting the painstaking and deliberate effort required to draw, paint, or sculpt our own visions of sacred images or life events may encourage spiritual perceptions that might otherwise remain hidden from us.

Perhaps we need to embark upon or spend more time with our spiritual journaling or reading.

Maybe our prayer time has become lethargic. Do we need to invest some energy and movement into our prayer time?

This is where an experienced spiritual director is a real help. God is constantly calling us to a deeper intimacy with Him. Find a way to respond.

Meditative Prayer

The Rosary, taught to Catholics in childhood, is a meditative prayer form that leads to contemplative prayer. It is comprised of 20 decades of Hail Mary's said while meditating on the mysteries surrounding the life of Christ. These mysteries are the Joyful, the Sorrowful, the Luminous, and the Glorious.

Many people don't know that the Rosary prayers of the Our Father and Hail Mary date back to the early Christians and the apostles. The Rosary was developed by the early Christians in imitation of the more educated people who read the Psalms in response to God's Old Testament command for an offering in the morning and evening.

Psalms in the Book of David numbered 150, so these early Christians developed a system of saying 150 Hail Mary's. This was referred to as Our Lady's Psalter.

Our Lady appeared to St. Dominic in 1214 and told him that she wished him to make the Rosary known as a remedy to the Albigensian[3] heresy which was gaining popularity in those times. St. Dominic became devoted to the Rosary and preached it strongly throughout his life. It remains a mainstay in Dominican traditions.

Around 1460, Blessed Alan de la Roche was also visited by Our Lady who told him to also spread devotion to the Rosary.

In the 20th Century she again appeared, this time to the children at Fatima and told them to tell people to say the Rosary every day to obtain peace for the world.

Pope Pius X stated that the Holy Rosary was the most favored devotion for miracles.

St Louis de Montfort declared that the Rosary is a priceless treasure inspired by God.

Catholic theologians tell us it is considered the greatest prayer in the church after the Mass and the Liturgy of the Hours.

Our Lady made 15 promises for those who have devotion to the Holy Rosary (see appendix). She gave these promises to St. Dominic and to Blessed Alan de le Roche.

Lectio Divina (Sacred Reading) is a meditative prayer, a form of which was first practiced by the ancient Jewish peoples. It was adopted by the Desert Fathers and Mothers in the early days of the church, and later adapted for group use by monasteries in the Middle Ages.

I was excited to realize that I was learning a prayer form that had been used by the Desert Fathers and Mothers. It felt like I was reaching back in time and connecting to people very close to God. Years later, I came to understand that the Jewish people had been praying the scriptures for centuries. I felt awestruck to realize that the Blessed Mother and St. Joseph would have instructed the young Jesus in this method of prayer.

That information connected me to the certainty that in praying Lectio Divina I was actually engaging in the same prayer form that Jesus Christ, my Saviour, would have prayed.

To me, Lectio Divina became a special and sacred way of praying.

Another way to refer to Lectio Divina is praying with the scriptures and it is an excellent way to begin one's journey into contemplative prayer.

The individual practice of Lectio Divina would begin with a prayer to the Holy Spirit asking for guidance and grace in your prayer time. Then study Holy Scripture until you find a word, phrase, or passage that speaks to your heart.

Spend some time with that scripture, think about it, repeat it several times, probe its meaning for the moment you are in, question how its message might affect your present life. In other words, ponder this scripture, meditate on it until you feel very comfortable with its meaning for you. A prayer to God thanking Him for this inspiration would be a natural next step.

Talk to God for a while until you can't think of anything else to say. Then be quiet. Rest in the Lord's presence. Be open to the Lord's speaking to your heart. As Mother Theresa often said, "God speaks to the silent heart."

Groups of like-minded individuals can do Lectio Divina together. There is great power in group meditation.

In the Middle Ages as monasteries flourished, spiritual leaders developed a step-by-step format for the monks to pray Lectio Divina together, a practice which continues today.

CULTIVATING A LIFE OF PRAYER

The group leader begins with a prayer to the Holy Spirit for guidance , openness, and growth in one's spirit. A scripture passage is read. Participants listen to the scripture and chose a word or phrase that seems to touch their souls. Usually they will take turns sharing that word with each other.

In the second step, the scripture will then be read again while the participants listen with their hearts and minds for deeper meanings of the words they have chosen. After a few moments of meditation on this scripture and their chosen word some members of the group might wish to share a deeper meaning of their word or phrase which has occurred to them.

In the third step, the scripture will be read again by the group leader after which there will be a few minutes of silence as the individuals form a prayer within themselves to God.

As a fourth step, the group leader will suggest that it is time to begin listening with their hearts to what Jesus might be trying to say to them. At this time there will be several minutes of silent listening.

Typically there is no sharing of either their prayers to God or the results of their listening to God. However, in groups I've been in, participants are often eager to discuss the perceptions they have experienced, often resulting in fruitful discussions.

As a fifth step, the individuals go about their life with the advice to think about the word throughout the day, pondering it, praying about it, and seeing how that word can become part of who they are in the future.

I have found that it is wise to keep a journal of these experiences so that you can revisit the path of your spiritual growth. The path of spiritual development can be rocky at times and it is human to feel times of dryness or unworthiness.

Other times you may feel that you have been overwhelmed by the busyness of your life and you feel that you have made no headway in becoming a more spiritual person. At such times, a journal that details your spiritual journey can be very reassuring and inspirational

The step from meditative prayer to contemplative prayer is a natural progression over time and happens so quietly that many people do not realize that their soul has taken that step.

Often times people think they have fallen asleep during their prayers and they may feel frustrated at their lack of will power. I have heard more than one person complain that they often seem to fall asleep while meditating on the prayers and mysteries of the rosary. I believe a more likely explanation is that their souls have been in communion with their God and Savior, Jesus Christ.

I ask "How long were you 'asleep?'" If it's several hours, I acknowledge that must have been sleep. If it's twenty minutes or so, if your eyes open with enough time to peacefully arrange to be at your next appointment, I assume some part of yourself has slipped into a deeper prayer than that in which you were consciously participating.

Contemplative Prayer

When a praying person is ready, they will feel drawn to contemplative prayer. Once we have felt this desire, it is important to dedicate part of our prayer time to contemplative prayer. But what is contemplative prayer?

Contemplative prayer is sitting quietly with God, beyond words and thoughts. It is simply being with the One Who Loves Us and loving back. We've all experienced a similar state with another person at some time in our lives when we felt so comfortable being with that person that there was no need for words.

Reaching such a place with God is not easy. This isn't because God isn't there. God is. But in our humanness our minds just want to keep thinking about something, anything. It is difficult to relax so completely that we can reach that quiet place where we can finally listen to the quiet voice of God.

Many methods have been suggested to help people contemplate. The truth is that sitting quietly, relaxing, gazing at a religious symbol such as a cross or a statue or picture of the Lord, and wanting to talk with God, or meditating on some aspect of his word, will in time lead us into His Presence.

The desire to be with God is deep within our hearts. When we become aware of that yearning, God is thrilled! He is calling us and we are responding. He will lead us, step by step, into His Presence. He will talk to our hearts. Be patient and trust.

I like to prepare for contemplative prayer with spiritual reading for a short time. I prefer a very quiet atmosphere but I know that soft, instrumental music can be helpful to many people. After allowing myself to relax, I pray to the Holy Spirit for help in getting my mind and heart ready for prayer. Sitting quietly, I stop the racing of thoughts in my mind by repeating the name of Jesus, or a short aspiration such as "Jesus, I love you" or "Lord, have mercy."

One of the difficulties in mental prayer is that as we relax and move into a still place of prayer, situations in our lives that are troubling us may float into our minds. We may feel helpless to rid ourselves of these thoughts, or to solve the problems that have surfaced.

As these thoughts and problems enter your mind, turn them over to God to solve. Admit your helplessness and release them to God. No matter how long or how often they surface, do not try to solve these problems. Don't struggle with them. Let them slide away from your consciousness.

People often don't realize how much Jesus loves them and how much he wants to strengthen their love for him. They know their human weaknesses and their struggle to be faithful. Then they think of the great saints of the church and cannot imagine themselves in the company of such holy people. It is hard for an individual who feels that way to imagine that God is visiting them personally, and spending time conversing with their souls. Such an event may be beyond their capacity to even consider.

But if Jesus is willing to come to us in Holy Communion, why is it so impossible to believe that he joins us when we are praying to him? I do believe that all Christians are called to contemplative prayer. We just need to believe that Jesus loves us enough to want to commune with us.

[3]Albigensian heresy flourished in France in the 12th and 13th centuries. These people believed in a dual nature of man: the material world and the human body created by the devil and inherently evil and the soul created by God and inherently good. Among their beliefs, they denied that Jesus Christ or the Holy Spirit were God because of the human body of Jesus which indicated they were part of the material world. They denied the resurrection of the body at the final judgement, or eternal punishment. They did not believe in the Sacraments or marriage. Because of these beliefs, they advocated perpetual celibacy to stop procreation, suicide was condoned to liberate the soul from the body, and they practiced abstention from all animal meat except fish.

11 *Spiritual Guidance*

Spiritual direction helps us respond to the invitation from Jesus to have a deeper relationship with him, and helps us more accurately discern where the Holy Spirit is leading us. While aware of the problems of evil, spiritual direction focuses on the positive aspects of the world.

The need for a praying person to have a spiritual guide is important. It is quite likely that a person with an active prayer life will find themselves confused at times about their progress. They may need some discernment clarifying experiences they are having and may feel the need to share with a trusted person who has also embraced a life of prayer.

The Sacrament of Confession is an excellent source of spiritual guidance if you can develop a relationship with your confessor. With the current shortage of priests, it's the rare priest who is willing to hear the "small stuff" you've done or provide guidance. If you do find such a priest consider him a treasure and go back to him.

Comfort and peace comes when we follow the path laid down by Jesus Christ. The Ten Commandments and the Sermon on the Mount give us the tools for living in the world and having eternal life.

It would have been difficult, impossible, for Jesus to talk to the people of his day in terms of what we know today. He had to give us directions for how to live within out human frailties and be at peace with ourselves and our neighbors. He knew the ramifications of stress, anger, and resentment on our bodies and the spiritual and physical health problems that would result.

He couldn't explain it to the people of his day because they would never have understood what he was talking about. Cancer, glial cells, memory banks, receptor sites, addictions, neuronal firing, muscle tension, gastric distresses, inflammation, high blood pressure – these words would have meant nothing to people in 33 AD.

Jesus told us how to live. He gave us the commandments to love God and to love our neighbor as we loved ourselves. He gave us the Beatitudes. He told us to forgive each other 7 times 77 times. Jesus also told us that the way to Heaven was through him – to live as he was instructing us. He told us that we needed to become as little children to gain Heaven.

He essentially told us to accept his directions for living and to obey those directions with the simplicity of a child being told not to run in the street or reach for hot pans on the stove.

Jesus knew our spirituality would be worked out through our minds and emotions – both of which are vulnerable to being deceived. Some of us are bright intellectually and some of us are less so, but the path to Heaven is the same for all.

Jesus gave us directions for walking the path that everyone could follow if they were as obedient as little children, even when the directives didn't make sense to us in our scientific and progressive world, or if, in our particular life circumstances, following his counsel would cause us much emotional pain.

So while we may feel other behavior would be more logical, we need to believe that He loved us, knew what was best for us physically as well as spiritually, and what would keep us out of mental struggles with evil. When you consider his words, the Bible stands out as a strong source of spiritual direction.

Finding a personal spiritual director may feel like a challenge. It is not necessary to have a priest as a spiritual director, especially these days with the shortage of priests, but thankfully there are praying people everywhere.

Many communities have developed programs teaching religious and lay people with the necessary prayer life and talents the skills to become spiritual directors. Check with those local religious communities who have developed spiritual direction programs for referrals, or call your local diocese.

Additionally, many books are available which will help to guide us in the spiritual life and lead us in prayer. Among them are such classics as:

- The New Testament Writers
- The Franciscan and Dominican Writers
- The Desert Fathers
- The Mystics of the Middle Ages
- The Great Schools of the Middle Ages
- St Catherine of Sienna
- The Spanish Mystics
- Thomas Merton
- Henry Nouwan
- Browse in a Catholic Bookstore. There will be a book that will call out to you.
- There is a short list of readings at the back of this book which have been helpful to me and which are easy to find.

Don't discount the influence of your friends. It is important to interact with prayerful people often so choose your friends wisely. You may gain much wisdom and support from your interactions with them.

12 *Spiritual Reading*

This world pushes our senses and intensifies our desire for gratifications. Additionally, the modern world deifies excitement and a constant increase in physical and mental stimulation.

Daily reading of scripture and other spiritual books will keep us in touch with the reality of our personal goals and the important priorities in our lives.

Spiritual reading will set a tone for the entire rest of our lives. It can uplift our faith as we read of the activities of other people who have sought a deeply prayerful life and found a friendship with God. Such reading can elevate our consciousness and keep our activities in line with our objectives for ourselves.

The lives of the Saints brings actual human beings and their struggles to overcome the temptations of this world into focus for us so that we don't feel so alone in our own battles. It clarifies their insights into the spiritual world and shares their patterns of prayer for us to emulate.

Such reading will also help us to develop an understanding of the theology of our faith. It can answer many questions that may have lain in the back of our minds for years.

As you prepare for spiritual reading, as before any other spiritual activity, take a few minutes to relax and focus on what you are preparing to do. Pray that the Holy Spirit will give you an understanding of what you are reading and how it can bring meaning to your life today.

If you are able to find like-minded people, join (or start!) a Christian book club where you read and then discuss together the book you have all read. This can add a depth of understanding which you might have missed with only your own interpretation of what the author was trying to convey to readers.

13 *Spiritual Journaling*

Keeping a spiritual journal allows the individual – and perhaps their spiritual director if they care to share – to observe the Lord's activity in their life. It is also a source of self-knowledge and can be healing to one's spiritual and emotional life. A journal shows trends in our past and present and possibly our future. It is a tool to notice things, both positive and negative, that are happening that we might normally overlook.

Journaling attunes us to our own needs so that we know what to expect from ourselves in relationships, in our spiritual lives, and in how we are reacting to the problems in our daily lives. It is a place to say who we really are and how we really feel about things.

The key to a spiritual journal is honesty. This honesty opens us and allows God entrance to us at our core where change is possible. When we name what holds us back from carrying out our intentions, we can give it to God. In our weakness and our "neediness" is where Christ wants to meet us and heal us.

It is important to remember that what we write is not as important as how we are feeling as we write. When we recognize the feeling, it is important to acknowledge it and express it in writing as fully as possible. Owning our feelings helps us become aware of our motivations in situations and relationships and can lead us to greater growth both emotionally and spiritually. It can allow us to ask for God's healing in areas where we may not have been aware that support was needed.

Writing is a way of learning. Our writing can become negative as we confront certain issues buried deep within ourselves, such as expressing a feeling of helplessness in dealing with some aspect of our personality. It's a good thing that we face such a concern, but if we stop writing at this point we can imprint that perception on our minds and end our session feeling defeated.

So if we do encounter a time when our writing leads us to a place that needs healing, always continue to write, ending the journaling with positive thoughts.

Such thoughts could be a written plan to deal with our problem, or it could be a written prayer to God to give us the wisdom and the strength to deal with our issue. This allows us to end our journal entry learning a positive solution to our concern, and feeling optimistic about our future.

14   *Methods of Journaling*

There are many ways to journal. Some folks like to just write whatever appeals to them to write at the time. However, with spiritual journaling we want to focus on the action of God in our lives. Any of the four methods suggested below will help to keep our mind on our spiritual growth.

Stay with each method for several days, perhaps a couple of weeks, then move to another method for a similar amount of time. After attempting each method, think about them prayerfully and determine if one or another suits your needs at this time better than another and stay with that method for a significant amount of time. Shift to another method when you feel called to do so or your spiritual director suggests it is time to change.

Remember to relax and calm your mind before starting your journaling.

Remember to say a prayer to the Holy Spirit for wisdom in understanding your spiritual journey and to guide your writing and your thoughts.

Method #1

Write briefly what is has felt like to be you today. Make it a statement of your union with God. How was your prayer time? Or did you skip it? Why? How did you feel about yourself during the day?

Have you had interactions with other people that were pleasant, unpleasant, confusing, deceitful, joyful, spiritual? How did you contribute to the tone of the interaction? Did you ask God's help during negative meetings? Did you find yourself talking to God about your day during your day?

Method #2

Let a prayer flow out of you to God. Relate to your Creator. Let your prayer be free flowing and spontaneous. How does it make you feel to write this prayer to God?

Method #3

Open your bible and read with a prayerful mind. When you have found a few lines of scripture that seem very meaningful to you, write them down and where you found them. Pray about them. Relate them to your own life. Think about the different ways you might have handled a certain situation if this scripture had been a part of your life then.

Start writing your thoughts about the scripture verse and let it gradually turn into a prayer to the Almighty. Keep that verse in your mind for the next few days as you go about your life. Notice where you find use for it and how it changes your life.

<u>Method #4</u>

Write briefly of the significant persons, events, places and scriptures of the day. How did the Word of God come to you today? How did you feel throughout the day?

After you have written in your journal using any of these methods, pause and put down your pen. Have a regular amount of time set aside, perhaps ten minutes. Pray quietly and then listen. Be still. Give the Lord time to tell you how He felt about your day and you.

Look for God's view of your day and the events in it. Imagine what He would say and how very unlike our mind His observations might be. Let Jesus tell you that He loves you. Let Him call you to trust and hope.

Every day has a mystery, a secret just for us. Writing about our day, praying over it with God and letting Him talk with us while we listen helps us capture the lesson the Lord would have us learn.

Then take the time to write those thoughts down that you have understood in your meditation. You will want to study them many times in your lifetime.

15 *A Few Last Words*

In one of my meetings with Fr. Kane on Living a Life of Prayer, he said the following words to me. I wrote them down immediately and have found inspiration from them throughout my life. I would like to share them with you.

"In a life of prayer there will be days when we come before the Lord dumbly with a mind that feels vacant and a heart that feels nothing. That is OK. All prayer is a progression to wisdom. Prayer is a little of dying to self. It is not always easy. That's OK too.

"Hold fast to your dream of cultivating a life of prayer, of finding a greater depth of closeness with Jesus. Maintain your prayer times. Stay with your decision and the path to Jesus that you have chosen. The most difficult days in prayer are when our structure is most strengthened."

The Law of Life Prayer: "Lord, be gentle with us but do not spare us as we want to grow to be like you."

Rev. John Kane, C.Ss.R. 1984

16 *Helpful Spiritual Resources*

Books

Catherine of Siena, The Dialogue, Suzanne Noffke, OP, 1980, Paulist Press, New York

Come Away My Beloved, Frances J. Roberts, The King's Press, Ojai, Ca, 1970, latest edition 2013

Difficulties in Mental Prayer, Fr. M. Eugene Boylan, Monk of the Cistercian Abbey of Mount St. Joseph, Roscrea, The Newman Press, Westminster, Md. 1944, latest edition 2014, revised

Discovering Pathways to Prayers, Msgr. David E. Rosage, Living Flame Press, 1975

Finding Peace in Pain: Sharing the Passion of Christ, Yvonne Hebert, Living Flame Press, 1984, Amazon Press 2015

In My Own Words, Mother Theresa, compiled by Jose Luis Gonzalez-Balado, Liguori Publications, Liguori, Missouri, 1997

Introduction to the Devout Life, St. Francis de Sales, 1st Ed. 1609, US Publisher: Vintage Books, latest edition 2013

Jesus, The Bridegroom: The Greatest Love Story Ever Told, Brant Pitre, Image Publishing, 2014

Man's Search for Meaning, 1st Ed. 1946, Victor Frankl, Simon & Schuster's Pocket Books, last printing in 2014.

My Way of Life, *Pocket Ed of St. Thomas, (Simplified Summa Theologica)* W. Farrell, OP and M. Healy, STD, Confraternity of the Precious Blood, Brooklyn, NY, 1952

Nature and Grace, Karl Rahner, SJ, Sheed and Ward, NY, 1964

Pilgrim Souls, A Collection of Spiritual Autobiographies, Editors: Amy Mandelker & Elizabeth Powers, Simon & Schuster, NY, 1999

Prayer is a Hunger, Edward Farrell, STL, Dimension Books, Denville, NJ, 1972

Prayer, Our Deepest Longing, Ronald Rolheiser, Franciscan Media, Cincinnati, Oh., 2013

Praying with John of the Cross, Wayne Simsic, Saint Mary's Press, Christian Brothers Publications, Winona, Minn., 1993

Rethinking Forgiveness for Christians, Yvonne Hebert, Amazon Press, 2015

The Secret Strength in Depression, 3rd Ed., Frederick Flack, MD, Hatherleigh Press, 2002

What is Contemplation? Thomas Merton, Templegate Publishers, Springfield, Ill., 10th Printing, 1981, latest edition 2013

Periodicals:

Spiritual Life: A Quarterly of Contemporary Spirituality Published by the Discalced Carmelites in Washington, DC, 20002 since 1955.   Beginning in 2015, only back copies are available in print. Spiritual Life is now published as an e-journal. There is no charge to receive it on-line.
http://www.spiritual-life.org. (1-888-616-1713)

Weavings: A Journal of the Christian Spiritual Life, by The Upper Room, Nashville, Tn, **www.upperroom.org/weavings**

17   *The 15 Promises of Our Lady*

These promises were made by the Blessed Mother to St. Dominic and to Blessed Alan de la Roche.

1. Whoever shall faithfully serve me by the recitation of the Rosary, shall receive powerful graces.
2. I promise my special protection and the greatest graces to all those who shall recite the Rosary.
3. The Rosary shall be a powerful armor against hell. It will destroy vice, decrease sin, and defeat heresies.
4. It will cause virtue and good works to flourish; it will obtain for souls the abundant mercy of God; it will withdraw the hearts of people from the love of the world and its vanities, and will lift them to the desire of eternal things. Oh, that souls would sanctify themselves by this means.
5. The soul which recommends itself to me by the recitation of the Rosary, shall not perish.
6. Whoever shall recite the Rosary devoutly, applying himself to the consideration of its Sacred Mysteries shall never be conquered by misfortune. God will not chastise him in His justice, he shall not perish by an unprovided death; if he be just, he shall remain in the grace of God, and become worthy of eternal life.
7. Whoever shall have a true devotion for the Rosary shall not die without the Sacraments of the Church.

8. Those who are faithful to recite the Rosary shall have during their life and at their death the light of God and the plentitude of His graces; at the moment of death they shall participate in the merits of the Saints in Paradise.

9. I shall deliver from purgatory those who have been devoted to the Rosary.

10. The faithful children of the Rosary shall merit a high degree of glory in Heaven.

11. You shall obtain all you ask of me by the recitation of the Rosary.

12. All those who propagate the Holy Rosary shall be aided by me in their necessities.

13. I have obtained from my Divine Son that all the advocates of the Rosary shall have for intercessors the entire celestial court during their life and at the hour of death.

14. All who recite the Rosary are my children, and brothers and sisters of my only Son, Jesus Christ.

15. Devotion of my Rosary is a great sign of predestination.

"The Rosary is a certain formula of prayer, which is made up of twenty decades of ten "Hail Mary'0s" with an "Our Father" before each decade, and in which the recitation of each decade is accompanied by pious meditation on a particular mystery of our Redemption. (Roman Breviary) The name "Rosary," however, is commonly used in reference to only a fourth part of the twenty decades."

Source: theholyrosary.org

CPSIA information can be obtained
at www.ICGtesting.com
Printed in the USA
LVOW04s1016130316

478975LV00017B/607/P

God's Armor:
Bulwark Against the Devil's Tactics

"Grow strong in the Lord with the strength of His power. Put God's armor on, so as to be able to resist the devil's tactics. For it is not against human enemies that we have to struggle, but against the Sovereignties and the Powers who originate the darkness in this world, the spiritual army of evil in the heavens. That is why you must rely on God's armor, or you will not be able to put up any resistance when the worst happens, or have enough resources to hold your ground.

So stand your ground, with truth buckled around your waist, and integrity for a breastplate, wearing for   shoes on your feet the eagerness to spread the gospel of peace and always carrying the shield of faith so that you can use it to put out the burning arrows of the evil one. Then you must accept salvation from God to be your helmet and receive the Word of God from the Spirit to use as a sword. Pray all the time, asking for what you need, praying in the Spirit on every possible occasion."

Ephesians 6:10-18   The Jerusalem Bible, 1968

How can 'truth' be a belt?'   Study the bible, the Ten Commandments, The Papal Encyclicals, and other spiritual writings until your understanding of God's word becomes sustenance for your very being, the girding supporting your body's vulnerable center.

Why the emphasis on 'integrity?' Follow the Word of God without the slightest deviation and no evil can penetrate your heart to affect your emotions or leave your decisions and behavior vulnerable to a lack of wisdom which could ultimately redirect your steps toward evil. Following God's law with integrity proves that you have the desire to avoid idols in your life and doesn't give the devil a foothold to tempt you.

How can shoes be armor? If you are preaching the Word of God, giving the example of living the Word of God, we will experience added strength to walk in the footsteps of Jesus Christ.

Why is faith referred to as a shield? If the strength of our faith has become a virtue, a spiritual gift, our faith no longer needs reason to defend or explain it. Our faith becomes impenetrable in the face of argument, the logic of a non-believer, or the assaults of demons.

What makes salvation a helmet? Living by t
means that we have accepted God's covena
salvation. This promise of salvation protects
minds from the effects of ill-conceived spirit
curiosity, emotions, and evil-inspired assaul

How can the "Word" be a sword?   God's W
the Spirit, can and does cut through the dec
temptations of the demons to reveal truth t
to see it.

Always a powerful weapon, prayer can be e\
when we ask and allow the Holy Spirit to pra
our needs.

All of God's armor works together to protect
with evil forces. To rely on some   pieces of ;
discarding other articles of armor as too diffi
unimportant, leaves us vulnerable to attacks

An additional weapon is the Sign of the Cross
reverence and an understanding that this sig
your loyalty and love for Jesus Christ and the
trust in the protection this belief gives you.